I0539988

Come! Let's
Evangelize

Come! Let's Evangelize

Dr. Sharon Forde-Atikossie

CITI OF BOOKS

Copyright © 2025 by Sharon Forde Atikossie

All rights reserved. No part of this publication may be reproduced, distributed, or transmitted in any form or by any means, including photocopying, recording, or other electronic or mechanical methods, without the prior written permission of the copyright owner and the publisher, except in the case of brief quotations embodied in critical reviews and certain other noncommercial uses permitted by copyright law. For permission requests, write to the publisher, addressed "Attention: Permissions Coordinator," at the address below.

CITIOFBOOKS, INC.
3736 Eubank NE Suite A1
Albuquerque, NM 87111-3579
www.citiofbooks.com
Hotline: 1 (877) 389-2759
Fax: 1 (505) 930-7244

Ordering Information:

Quantity sales. Special discounts are available on quantity purchases by corporations, associations, and others. For details, contact the publisher at the address above.

Printed in the United States of America.

ISBN-13:   Softcover   979-8-89391-663-8
              eBook   979-8-89391-664-5

Library of Congress Control Number: 2025908671

Table of Contents

MY STORY

Someone approached me as I was walking out of a visiting church's conference and asked, "So when are you going to open your church?"

I immediately pointed my finger to the heavens and looked up saying "Hope this is not you sending this person to me, because the answer is still no. My husband is dead, and maybe you would send me another helper to do your work, but the answer is still no. I do not need any headaches; just want to have a peaceful life to rejoice in your name, and to draw souls to you the best way I know."

What is this nonsense about opening church when this visiting church that I am now leaving has only five members and is struggling to understand how to evangelize? I do not even know how to help them because all churches evangelize differently!

However, not long after, while traveling on a mission trip, I went with the intent to preach the gospel, fellowship with some of the church members, and return home, however, I was confronted by a few pastors' who met me at the airport in South America, and made it plain that they need help evangelizing.

Of course, and all of them were looking to me for answers, and I had nothing at that moment. I was going to try from the internet since I was not totally prepared to evangelize, but, with my luck, there was no electricity available to use the internet.

As I lay in my hotel room that night, I began to think and try to remember everything that I was taught about evangelism. I had to pray and ask God for a lot of help because I had no intention of embarrassing myself; the next day, some members along with the pastors would be waiting for a reply.

Thank God for the teaching I received, the learning, and my faith. I was able to explain that evangelism is not only just walking up to someone and telling them about Jesus, they have to use wisdom such has forming a conversation, finding a common ground, being pleasant, dress in a way where they will blend in.

I was able to explain additional tips on what the evangelist needs to know prior to going out to evangelize, such as knowing the gospel, knowing how to pray, learning to adapt to their environment, moving in the power, winning souls, and to remind them to observe their environment prior to approaching someone to tell them about Jesus.

TO THE EVANGELIST

Dear Evangelist,

I learned that as a Christian evangelist, is very important to the church, and to the body of Christ. It is where they are to fulfill the core command from Jesus Christ which is to make disciples of all nations and to share the good news of salvation.

It is showing and telling with both word and deed who Jesus is and how it's possible to have a relationship with Him. It is the privilege of entering into the spiritual journey of another person, discovering how God is at work and the role that we can play.

It sounds so simple in theory. So why does it seem so hard to do?

If you are like most motivated Christians, you genuinely desire to share your faith in Jesus, and all that He has done for you, but the thought of it may excite and terrify you at the same time.

The desire to share one's faith is a natural overflow of one's relationship with Jesus Christ; however, when a person in love rarely stops thinking and talking about the object of their affection, that person who has genuinely experienced who Jesus Christ is expressing a similar compulsion (Acts 4:20). 20 "As for us, we cannot help speaking about what we have seen and heard."

Sadly enough, evangelism is not just a process of explaining the truth until another person understands, and then they automatically make the choice to believe in Jesus. They have all sorts of barriers, or obstacles to overcome before they accept the truth about God, and He is more than just a series of concepts for one to either agree or disagree with.

One must always remember that God is real; He is alive. He lives in all of us, for He said the one way a relationship with Him can work is by trusting Him to be our ultimate authority. Proverbs 3:5-6 "Trust in the Lord with all your heart and lean not on your own understanding; in all your ways submit to him, and he will make your paths straight."

It is not surprising that people who are self-protective and independent often resist the truth about God. Those who do not yet believe in God are only half of the way, which is why evangelism is complicated.

If you are a Christian who has a desire to share what you believe with someone else, you have to choose to take a step of faith. Fear, anxiety and nervousness are very normal as you learn how to make evangelism as part of your everyday life. You cannot know how the person you're talking to will react or how it might change your relationship with them.

Understand that this is the crucial word in this situation. If you are willing to learn how to share your faith and willing to trust God with the outcomes, then you're ready to begin.

As the Author, David Geisler explain that one must understand "what makes old models of witnessing ineffective in today's culture; why evangelism must start with relational pre-evangelism; how to ask questions, listen attentively, and understand what someone believes; ways to identify the real barriers to belief in order to build a bridge to truth, and how to keep dialogue going with different personality types, also we must remember that there are different types, and forms of evangelism, and wisdom is the key to evangelizing regardless of where you are.

Sincerely,

Sharon FordeAtikossie

Pastor Dr. Sharon Forde-Atikossie

WOULD IT BE YOU

The singer Mr. Marvin Winans sang a song, by the name of "Who is going to tell them," and a part of the song states

"Who is gonna to tell them Jesus love them
Who is gonna to tell them that there is a better way
Who is gonna warn them of the things coming on them
So, God can turn their nights to day
Somebody has to warn them
Somebody has to tell them"

My question to you the reader, would it be you the evangelist,
is going to tell them?
Will you be a true servant of God?
Would you be the one to say "Yes Lord send me…?
Then I pray that you submit your lives to Christ
Get to know the gospel in order to evangelize
Know how to pray in spirit and in truth
Have the ability to adapt
To move in the power of Jesus Christ
And win the soul to Christ!

THE MISSION OF THE EVANGELIST

I have decided to get straight to the point regarding this topic. This is because, upon observation and survey, there's an urgent need to reach many people in the world who don't know Jesus and don't know to whom they should give thanks to, also to those who claim to be saved and are children of God who wants to share the blessings they have experienced.

If we are enjoying God's goodness, and I include myself in that why aren't we proclaiming it from the rooftops?

Are we operating in a selfish manner? Why not reach out to our brothers and sisters and give them a chance to experience the goodness of God? Let us bring them to church so they can learn more about Him. To do this effectively, there are several things an evangelist must know and learn.

An evangelist is a person who is called by God to spread the gospel. They are like a newscaster on television or a journalist writing for a newspaper, except that the evangelist's message never changes.

I learn that in Acts 18 explain "that when the Holy Spirit comes upon us we receive power and become witnesses and it's not just any power it's a godly boldness a divine courage that makes us want to share the gospel with everyone around us.

One gets that irresistible urge to talk about Jesus. There is this burning desire which does not come from ourselves, but from the Holy Spirit driving us.

God places in our hearts a deep love for the lost which is having compassion that makes us see people differently, then suddenly the idea of keeping this good news to ourselves seems impossible.

We want everyone to know the love of Christ, and when we think of the disciples after Pentecost, we see that before they were timid and afraid of being persecuted, but after receiving the Holy Spirit they became bold preaching without fear of any consequence.

The evangelists' mission is to go beyond the four walls of the church, meeting people where they are, and proclaiming God's Word, simply and clearly explaining what God says about His Son, Jesus Christ, and what He has done for all. This must be done with urgency because people's souls are at stake.

Evangelists aren't simply to tell people about the Bible, but to share the Good News about God, which never changes. They must communicate it in a way that draws people in and makes them want to learn more about God and ask questions.

Their effectiveness depends on clearly and authoritatively preaching the Gospel from Scripture. "God said" and "Jesus spoke" are the authorities; not "I think," "we believe," or "our church teaches."

They must remember that God's Word alone is the authority, and it is more powerful than human or natural speaking ability.

The Bible is alive, active, and relevant (Hebrews 4:12) "For the word of God is alive and active. Sharper than any double- edged sword, it penetrates even to dividing soul and spirit, joints and marrow; it judges the thoughts and attitudes of the heart."

They are the most important ambassadors on earth, and it is not a calling just for the clergy, they are a mighty army with a calling to spread the gospel across the world, thereby having a vision to reach their own people and draw them to Christ.

If evangelists are unsure how to share their faith, whether face-to-face, through mail, media, or social media, and they must remember the following:

The Great Commission: Matthew 28:18-20, Jesus' command to "go therefore and make disciples of all nations."

The Salt and Light metaphor: Matthew 5:13-16, Christians are called to positively influence the world around them. Acts 1:8: The Holy Spirit empowers believers to witness to the ends of the earth.

Understanding that God is the one on mission to reach the world, and that the church participates in this work, is crucial.

Evangelists should address not only spiritual needs, but also social and physical needs, recognizing the cultural nuances of the community they are serving;

sharing their faith in one- on-one conversations; build relationships and sharing faith naturally through lifestyle; engage with the wider community through service and outreach initiatives; recognize that people are separated from God due to sin; understand that the death and the resurrection of Jesus is the only way to receive forgiveness and salvation; and respond to the Gospel by turning away from sin and trusting in Jesus Christ.

YOUR CHOICE

I learned that there is a difference in liking to do something, having a deep hunger and thirst for something, and having a calling to do something – all of these function is different.

In the case of someone who likes to do something, that person can easily change their mind, and look towards that next best attraction, because in order to like, there is that feeling of attraction; to regard; or to want something to include taking pleasure in something.

Having a hunger and thirst for something is to have an intense or desperate desire or craving or it is a deep and powerful yearning which propels one to aggressively seek out what they want until satisfied, where their feeling must be quenched.

Having a calling by God, is where God has allowed one to become the person, He created them to be, and for them to do the things He designed them to do, and this is where God will partner with one as they prayerfully move forward.

This process is a spiritual journey in which they will learn new things about themselves and about their relationship with the Lord and doing something significant beyond just personal needs.

These are just some of the requirements that one needs to become an Evangelist, to include knowledge, skills, and being able to identify the environment and culture.

WHO IS AN EVANGELIST

The word "evangelist" comes from the Greek words euaggélion (meaning "gospel") and euaggelistēs (meaning "evangelist").

2 Timothy 4:5 (NIV) 5 But you, keep your head in all situations, endure hardship, do the work of an evangelist, discharge all the duties of your ministry.

In the Bible, it explain that an evangelist is someone who proclaims good news, such as the gospel, and invites others to have a personal relationship with Jesus Christ, for they are individuals who seeks to convert others to the Christian faith so that they may be saved.

I learn that evangelists are often depicted with symbols that represent them, such as in Saint Matthew - The Angel; Saint Mark - The Lion; Saint Luke - The Ox, and Saint John - The Eagle and in the Christian tradition, the Four Evangelists are Matthew, Mark, Luke, and John, and they attributed with the creation of the four canonical Gospel accounts.

They are those who naturally relate to and connect with people that do not know or follow Jesus and having the ability to have one foot in the church and one foot in the world, and also, they are what one would call natural Bridge builders between two worlds.

They are those who seeks to convert others to the Christian faith so that they may be saved. This is often done through public preaching that involves spreading the gospel and calling on others to repent.

They also witness to Jesus's message and carry out his teachings in their everyday life. As we are instructed by Jesus in Mark 16:15-16 "Go into all the world and proclaim the gospel to the whole creation. Whoever believes and is baptized will be saved, but whoever does not believe will be condemned."

They are those who spend lots of time with people who don't follow Jesus; they love sharing the gospel and seem pretty natural doing so; they are regularly encouraging other believers to witness; they make themselves do evangelism; they believe in the exclusivity of the gospel and truth of eternal judgment; they hold themselves accountable to someone; they hold them accountable to doing evangelism as well; they pray for non- believers by name;

They often have a big heart that translates into local evangelism; they use the pulpit for evangelism, but they don't stop there; they tend to define "evangelism" narrowly (and properly, in my opinion); they grieve when they don't see lost persons get saved; they tend to be disciplined in Bible study and prayer; they humbly speak of their evangelistic attempts.

The main role of the evangelist is to share the gospel message of salvation and invite others to have a personal relationship with Jesus Christ.

As said before in the Christian tradition, the Four Evangelists are Matthew, Mark, Luke, and John, the authors attributed with the creation of the four canonical Gospel accounts, and. In the New Testament, they bear the titles: the Gospel of Matthew; the Gospel of Mark; the Gospel of Luke; and the Gospel of John.

They were witnesses to Jesus messages and carry out his teachings in their everyday life. As we are instructed by Jesus in Mark 16:15-16 "Go into all the world and proclaim the gospel to the whole creation. Whoever believes and is baptized will be saved, but whoever does not believe will be condemned."

QUALIFICATIONS OF AN EVANGELIST

To effectively fulfill the role of an evangelist, one needs a strong foundation of faith, a deep understanding of the Bible, a genuine love for Jesus, and a desire to help fellow believers achieve salvation.

An evangelist's role should not be self-appointed; rather, they should be appointed by a church leader, divinely guided by the Holy Spirit. The leader should recognize these qualities in the candidate:

They should have enthusiasm, thereby having a fervent desire to share faith in Jesus and inspire others to consider God.

The must show compassion, and having the ability to recognize a person's spiritual need and feel empathy for them.

Prayerfulness is a must, not just praying when they wake up, but be consistent in prayer, and reliance on God's guidance in convicting and converting individuals.

Holding oneself accountable, to include others accountable for effective evangelism.

Community Involvement by engaging with the local community and not isolating oneself.

Having a biblical foundation and having a disciplined approach to Bible study, while demonstrating a strong understanding of Scripture.

Having a deep, and sincere passion for evangelism, which must be evident in to all.

Showing humility, by speaking modestly about evangelistic efforts, attributing success to God.

Having a global, and international perspective on evangelist to include having a broad view of evangelism, in all cultures.

Showing of persuasion by having the ability to thoughtfully persuade people to consider faith choices.

Heir life Having a divine calling on their lives to spread the gospel, thereby drawing souls to Christ, especially to the ministry of evangelism.

Putting God first in everything they say or do, and being a true representative of God.

THE KEY TO EVANGELIZING

The key to evangelizing is not good preaching, it is prayer. The disciples never asked Jesus to teach them how to preach, they asked Him to teach them how to pray. They knew that's how He activated His power, and the evangelists can do the same.

Activating the power of the Holy Spirit to win souls will make your efforts surprisingly simple. After all, He can accomplish far more than we ever could on our own!

To do this, spend time meditating on God's Word and in intercessory prayer for those to whom you will minister.

These actions will bring about boldness in your witnessing. Plus, you won't lack for words when you've filled your heart with God's Word, and preparing the other man's heart by interceding and pulling down strongholds that would blind his mind (2 Corinthians 10:4-5).

If the Word is in you, it will make a way out. The Bible says to take no thought of how or what thing you will answer or what you will say, because the Holy Spirit will teach you in the same hour what you should say.

As you acquire a thorough knowledge of God's Word, then your Helper and Teacher, the Holy Spirit, will bring all things to your remembrance when you need it.

When we rise up as the local church and determine that we will fulfill the Great Commission, these seven surprisingly simple ways to evangelize will be important tools as some navigate evangelism for the first time.

We can make a great change in the world around us if each one will reach one with the gospel of Jesus Christ.

Additional keys to an evangelist are having a vision for reaching the community; teaching people to live out their faith; being the example, and getting everyone involved.

CHARACTERISTICS OF AN EVANGELIST

Charles Spurgeon, explain the seven characteristics of highly evangelistic Christians."

They are people of prayer. They realize that only God can convict and convert, and they are dependent upon Him in prayer. Most of the highly evangelistic Christians spend at least an hour in prayer each day.

They have a theology that compels them to evangelize. They believe in the urgency of the gospel message.

They believe that Christ is the only way of salvation.

They believe that anyone without Christ is doomed for a literal hell.

They are people who spend time in the Word. The more time they spend in the Bible, the more likely they are to see the lostness of humanity and the love of God in Christ to save those who are lost.

They are compassionate people. Their hearts break for those who do not have a personal relationship with Jesus Christ. They have learned to love the world by becoming more like Christ who has the greatest love for the world.

They love the communities where God has placed them. They are immersed in the culture because they desire for the light of Christ to shine through them in their communities.

They are intentional about evangelism. They pray for opportunities to share the gospel, and they look for those opportunities.

They are accountable to someone for their evangelistic activities.

That they must shows that they are persons of prayer, and have faith and believe that only God can convict and convert, and they are dependent upon God in prayer and in truth

That they must spend a lot of time in the Word, and the more time they spend in the Holy Bible, the Lord will show them and give them the direction on how to evangelize.

That they are a very compassionate for their where their hearts would break for those who do not have a personal relationship with God, and, they have to learn to love the world by becoming more like Christ who has the greatest love for the world.

That they must show the love for the communities where God has placed them. Where they will be immersed in the culture and be seen as the child of God, who have he the desire for the light of Christ to shine through them in their communities.

That they are intentional about evangelism.

That they know that they will be accountable to someone for their evangelistic activities, holding them accountable for their evangelistic efforts.

HOW TO EVANGELIZE

Know your message.

Build relationships of care and trust.

Ask deep questions.

Trust God to change hearts.

Be a willing, obedient witness.

Remember that eternal salvation is at stake.

Listen actively and communicate the Gospel message with humility and relevance.

Make evangelism personal by focusing on individuals.

Practice and build both skills and confidence.

Have a plan for helping new believers grow spiritually.

Proper preparation

Evangelize with more than one person

Appearance must match the environment

Speak the same language

Be vigilant

Stay focus in Christ

EVANGELISM

Evangelism changes lives!

In the case of evangelism - The way Jesus approached the woman at the well as stated in the bible (John 4) was not the same way he approached Zacchaeus (Luke 19).

They were different approaches, for He used wisdom in both cases, and with this in mine we see that Jesus met them where they are, and this is an example what real evangelism is.

The main goal of Evangelism is to lead others toward Jesus Christ through the path of salvation, which is through having faith belief in Jesus Christ, there by having the responsibility of the believers to share their faith and belief with others and inviting them to join the churches where they can learn more of the God they will serve.

For an evangelist they will meet the people wherever they are located, which is in different places all over the world, and the people, they are all different; their culture is different; their language is different; there are different age groups; there are those who do not know Christ; they are those who know of Christ; some may want to know of Him.

Some may not want to know of Him; some may want to challenge to Word of God; some may just want to totally reject what the evangelist has to say, and not forgetting they are those who has harden heart.

In addition to Jesus' own words about the importance of evangelism, His apostles said and did much the same. We know from the Book of Acts that after Christ's resurrection, the apostles were filled with the Holy Spirit and scattered across the land, preaching the word (Acts 8:4-25).

In Romans, the apostle Paul had spend time instructing the early church about the desperate need for evangelism so all can be saved. As Paul asks, "How, then, can they call on the One they have not believed in? And how can they believe in the One of whom they have not heard? And how can they hear without someone preaching to them?" (Romans 10:14).

As mention before, we learn that the term "Evangelism" is derived from the Greek word "euangelion." It means "gospel" or "good news."

Evangelism true meaning is known as Preaching the gospel. It is the act of spreading the gospel with the purpose of sharing the message of Jesus Christ which involves a deep commitment to Lord Jesus and a devotion to share your belief with others so that they feel inspired to act.

Evangelism is referred to activity "speaking the Good News that is the Good News of the Story of Jesus Christ suffering, death, and resurrection with the accompanying message of forgiveness, and eternal life through faith in him."

Evangelism is the deliberate attempt to impart religious beliefs and principles to inspire faith, conversion, or spiritual development.

Evangelism, on the other hand, is a phrase usually used to describe religious or ideological movements.

Evangelism describes the deliberate dissemination and advocacy of concepts, theories, or doctrines to win over new followers or converts.

Evangelism aims to reach a larger audience with a specific faith, ideology, or values. It includes preaching, teaching, proselytizing, and using persuasive communication tactics to persuade others of the benefits of a specific belief system.

Evangelism has different goals in religious contexts. Evangelism serves to baptize someone into a particular faith and mentor them toward salvation or spiritual development. It is used in ideological or social movements to mobilize support for a cause, promote societal change, or form a community of like- minded people who share a shared purpose.

Evangelism activities play a part in fostering a sense of community inside the church. Churches show their dedication to serving people and meeting societal needs by interacting with the larger community.

Evangelism, on the other hand, refers to a certain type of outreach that is commonly connected with religious or ideological movements. Evangelism focuses on actively advancing and disseminating certain doctrines, concepts, or beliefs to win followers or converts to a certain faith or philosophy.

The main goal of evangelism is to persuade people to adopt the evangelist's worldview, usually using preaching, teaching, and persuasive communication. It includes outreach activities.

Evangelism is done in many forms with the aim of drawing souls to Christ such as through personal witnessing; distributing Godly literature; preaching; taking part in mission trips; online evangelism; online invitations; online preaching along with other social media such as zoom, live streams, Facebook, and phone calls.

Some styles of evangelism are:

Direct evangelism:- This involves directly sharing the gospel with others, in most cases to more than one person at a time, and when doing so, one must be straightforward and focused on getting the message out, rather than building relationships or arguments.

They also guide the conversation toward a discussion about faith, without forcing the issue. An example of direct evangelism is Peter's address to the crowd at Pentecost in Acts 2.

Conversational Evangelism: This involves sharing one's faith in everyday conversations, it is sharing one's faith by engaging in natural, open-ended conversations with people, focusing on listening attentively, asking probing questions, and guiding the discussion towards the Gospel message in a non-confrontational manner, rather than delivering a pre-prepared speech.

It is using everyday interactions as opportunities to share one's beliefs organically, much like Jesus did in the Bible. He focus on listening by prioritizing, and understanding the other person's perspective and concerns before presenting your own beliefs; Ask open-ended questions while encouraging deeper conversation by asking questions that require more than a yes or no answer; have a natural flow where integrating of Integrate faith into everyday conversations, finding relevant connections to the topic at hand; seeking common ground by identifying and sharing values or experiences to build rapport before discussing spiritual matters; gentle proving thereby carefully guiding the conversation towards exploring spiritual issues without being overly forceful.

Intellectual Evangelism: This is where the evangelist uses logic, theology, philosophy, and apologetics to help people understand the Gospel message and believe in Jesus. Intellectual evangelists aim to remove intellectual barriers that might prevent people from accepting Christianity.

The evangelist must have an excellent knowledge and understanding of the Gospel. is a style of evangelism that focuses on engaging in thoughtful discussions and providing evidence and reasons for one's faith. Intellectual evangelists are expected to have a thorough understanding of the Gospel and be able to address intellectual roadblocks that may cause doubts about Christianity.

Testimonial Evangelism: This is where the evangelist will share their personal story of a Christian's faith journey, and how it impacted their life. It is a way to evangelize that is natural and conversational and can help others trust in Jesus. It also can be done where the evangelist can describe telling a story as a witness to what Christ has done in their lives. It is the story of the work of Christ in their life, or better yet share a bible story that come from the bible.

Relational Evangelism: This is a method of sharing the gospel by building relationships with people in your life, such as neighbors, co-workers, and friends. It can lead to effective discipleship and exponential growth.

It can also help you build stronger relationships in your community and emphasizes the advantages of building friendship relationships with unbelievers as a basis for sharing the gospel with them. Initial Contact Evangelism moves immediately into a gospel presentation, even with people we have met for the first time.

All of this involves building relationships (Focus on building genuine connections with people); Demonstrating Christ's love (Showing care for people through your actions and presence in their live); Sharing the gospel: (Sharing the gospel in the context of an existing relationship or while building a new one: Being yourself (One can witness to Christ by being yourself and sharing your faith without being trained or coerced); letting people know early – (To avoid awkwardness, let people know you are a follower of Jesus early in the relationship).

Invitational Evangelism: This is the practice of inviting people to attend the banquet that God has prepared which includes hospitality, networking, and having the desire to include others, they must be compassionate, thereby having the compassion as a motivation for evangelism; understand the good news: understand the good news of Jesus Christ; See people as God's children;: see lost people as people that God loves; rely on the Holy Spirit: rely on the power of the Holy Spirit; always invite: always give an invitation, and don't assume everyone in the room is a follower of Jesus; demonstrate care: demonstrate that you care about others and want their well-being through acts of service.

Service Evangelism: This is used by thousands of pastors and lay leaders to advance a style of evangelism that combines, it refers to a method of sharing one's faith by actively serving others through practical acts of kindness, demonstrating the love of Christ through deeds rather than solely through words, essentially using service as a way to connect with people and introduce them to the Gospel message; it's about showing compassion and meeting needs without expecting anything in return.

The Importance of Evangelism

It is the duty of every Christian to obey the Great Commission and preach to the non-believers, and the reason evangelism is important are:

In Evangelism, the main goal is to lead others toward the path of salvation which is through faith in Jesus. It is the responsibility of the believers to share their faith with others and make others join the kingdom of the lord which is referred to the activity of "speaking the Good News of Jesus Christ who suffered, die, and resurrection with the accompanying message of forgiveness, and eternal life through faith in him."

Evangelism is practiced in various forms, and these are:

Personal Witnessing – Witnessing, also called evangelism, is the work of individual Christians to share the Gospel of Jesus Christ with people in their everyday lives. It the act of sharing your personal experience with Jesus and what he has done for you with the goal of helping others have a relationship with Jesus. It is about letting Christ live through you and putting your transformation on display.

For Christians, witnessing is sharing your personal experience with Jesus. It might seem like a strange word to use in talking about your faith, but once you understand how the Bible uses the term, it makes a lot more sense, and becomes a meaningful part of your Christian life.

Before Jesus ascended, He gave His disciples some specific instructions. One of His most well-known imperatives has come to be known as the Great Commission:

"All authority in heaven and on earth has been given to me. Therefore, go and make disciples of all nations, baptizing them in the name of the Father and of the Son and of the Holy Spirit, and teaching them to obey everything I have commanded you. And surely, I am with you always, to the very end of the age" (Matthew 28:18b-20).

Here we see Jesus laying out His expectations for His followers. Disciples are to try to create more disciples in the world.

Distributing Literature – Handing out materials with the word of God, which talk about living for Christ

Preaching - Sharing the gospel is the act of sharing the good news of Jesus Christ with others

Taking Part in Mission Trips - Travelling and spreading the gospel to various places, encouraging those to surrender their life to Christ, and handing out small gifts.

Online Evangelism - Use the social media to encourage people to come to Christ, and to visit churches

There are five keys to an effective evangelism, and these are a vision for reaching the community; to teach people to live out their faith- this is done; be the example; get everyone involve. and offer multiple revivals.

The golden rule of Evangelism stated in the bible Matthew 7:122 So in everything, do to others what you would have them do to you, for this sums up the Law and the Prophets.

The message of the Evangelism is to Spread are teachings surround the death, burial, and resurrection of Lord Jesus. It also preaches on the forgiveness of sins and God's eternal life prophecy presented to those who have complete faith in Him.

It focuses on the desire to see others put faith in Jesus and experience the joy that they have already found through their unwavering faith.

Evangelism evolved as "Go therefore, and make disciples of all the nations, baptizing them in the name of the Father and of the Son and of the Holy Spirit"

This was the last command that Jesus gave us in Matthew 28:18-20. This command is called as "Great Commission," also known as Evangelism.

This command was given by Lord Jesus himself to his followers. He wanted his followers to share the good news of forgiveness, grace, and salvation. It would give rise to hope and uplift people who are without a savior. It would guide everyone to the path of light, the path of Jesus Christ.

Evangelism Is Important and it is the duty of every Christian to obey the Great Commission and preach the non-believers

The reasons why evangelism is important are:

Obey The Great Commission - As a believer in Lord Jesus, it is your primary task to obey the Great Commission. As the Lord himself commanded in Matthew 16:15, you are obliged to follow it and preach his teaching to others. He has commanded his followers to convert all the non-believers as disciples from all nations and baptize them.

Share Your Faith - As Jesus Christ himself commanded it, the "Great Commission" is considered the most significant Gospel message in Christianity. As a believer, you must consider it as an opportunity to share the message of salvation with others. It will not only reinstall your faith, but also lead others toward the holy path of salvation.

Leading Others - Evangelism is a means to lead others to the path of salvation, and this is the only path to getting closer to God and attaining eternity, this is considered an honorable act. By practicing evangelism, you get to guide others to heaven and bring them closer to Jesus Christ. Hence, share your message as much as you can.

Strengthen Other Evangelists - The preachings by one person can encourage fellow evangelists. It will motivate their beliefs and encourage them to work towards spreading the word of the Lord himself to the non-believers. Through this, each person can see how Gospel has the power to change the lives of the followers.

Resurrect The Community - The words of the Gospel act as a medium for transforming society. As the message in Gospel changes the nature of the people, this can lead to significant changes in the community, and it will lead to a positive society with less evil. Here, justice prevails, and everyone will work towards attaining salvation.

Express God's Love - Evangelism is a means to demonstrate the love of God and his compassion for others. As evangelists reaches out to more people, helping them, and share the word of hope and salvation through Lord Jesus, they are displaying God's love to others. Through this, they get closer to God and become a part of him.

Prepare For His Return - According to the Bible, Jesus Christ will return to build his kingdom on Earth. Evangelism is the main event that will shape the following events once Jesus Christ returns in the future. Every action of the evangelist is a step towards building the holy kingdom of Jesus Christ and awaiting his arrival.

The key to an effective evangelism is having a vision for reaching the community' teach people to live out their faith; be an example; get everyone involve and offer many different assistances when it comes to learning the word of God.

The golden rule of Evangelism is stated in Matthew 7:122 So in everything, do to others what you would have them do to you, for this sums up the Law and the Prophets.

What Message Does Evangelism Spread?

The main message and teachings surround the death, burial, and resurrection of Lord Jesus. It also preaches on the forgiveness of sins, and eternal life prophecy presented to those who have complete faith in Him.

It focuses on the desire to see others put faith in Jesus and experience the joy that they have already found through their unwavering faith.

Tony Evans explain that in that in Romans 3:23 " for all have sinned and fallen short of the glory of God, and most people will recognize that they have sinned in their lives that they have broken one of the ten commandments, or all of the ten commandments.

It would be rare that somebody doesn't recognize that they've done wrong in their lives so people need salvation because God is perfect, and he cannot accept imperfection, and all of us are imperfect we're sinners but that opens the door for Step 2 which is the good news the good news is in Romans 5:8 but, God demonstrated his own love for us in that while we were yet sinners.

Christ died for us, and the reason why that's good news is that God loves sinners, we are all our sinners, but God loves sinners so he loves all people particularly the person who you're talking to.

He loved them so much that he died on the cross Jesus Christ, God's son died on the cross to pay for their sins.

This is the bad news for all sinners but, the great news is God loves sinners, and he paid the price for every sinner which is everyone, since all have sinned.

So that means the person you're talking to can be reassured that God loves them no matter what sins they have committed, and that the sacrifice of Jesus Christ was a substitutionary payment for the sinners sin"

How Evangelism Evolve

Let us not be selfish in our walk with Jesus Christ, we want everyone to enjoy what we are enjoying, and that is living for Christ, and that is what He want from us, and that is "Go therefore, and make disciples of all the nations, baptizing them in the name of the Father and of the Son and of the Holy Spirit."

It was the last command that Jesus gave us in Matthew 28:18-20. This command is called as "Great Commission," also known as Evangelism. (Matthew 28:18-20) [18] Then Jesus came to them and said, "All authority in heaven and on earth has been given to me. [19] Therefore go and make disciples of all nations, baptizing them in the name of the Father and of the Son and of the Holy Spirit, [20] and teaching them to obey everything I have commanded you. And surely, I am with you always, to the very end of the age."

This command was given by Lord, Jesus Christ himself to his followers. He wanted his followers to share the good news of forgiveness, grace, and salvation. It would give rise to hope and uplift people who are without a savior. It would guide everyone to the path of light, the path of Jesus Christ.

Tools to Evangelize

In today's environment where there are constant changes only vehicles for evangelizing are needed.

Ingenuity has become vital, for everything seems to become digital, and vocal sounds which we all know as the social media, especially in North America and Europe. This form of communication allows one to reach millions of people at the same time.

However, one must find various ways on how to communicate such as vocalizing more, using illustrations, various messages, and other ways to grab the attention of the audience.

Preparation -Ask God guidance on where to evangelize, have a meeting with the ministry members, get their tools together to include pamphlets, it would be a great idea to check out the area first, make sure there are proper clearance which may include permits depending on the areas, make sure every knows the etiquette on greeting.

The evangelist should allow the bible to do most of their talking for them, and if they are not sure what to talk about, of how to explain, let the Bible do the work for them.

First the evangelist should ask their questions to the person they are talking to by having a simple casual conversation in a manner which they can draw the person's attention, bearing in mind that not all situations are the same, however some of the questions that the evangelist can ask are:

Do you have any kind of spiritual be?

If you died tonight, where would you go?

If what you were believing is not true, would you want to know?

The evangelist should try to change the conversation from the secular to the spiritual for them to be on the right track.

If the evangelist answers "yes" to the final question, they will have the opportunity of sharing their faith with them.

Instead of directly telling someone the Gospel in your own words, simply open the Bible and let God's Word speak for itself.

For this to work, the evangelist will need a Bible, and a few salvations passage to share,

Some passages that serve this purpose are listed below: And he died for all, that those who live should no longer live for themselves but for him who died for them and was raised again" (2 Corinthians 5:15).

"Here I am! I stand at the door and knock. If anyone hears my voice and opens the door, I will come in and eat with him, and he with me" (Revelation 3:20).

That if you confess with your mouth, 'Jesus is Lord,' and believe in your heart that God raised him from the dead, you will be saved. For it is with your heart that you believe and are justified, and it is with your mouth that you confess and are saved. As the Scripture says, 'Anyone who trusts in him will never be put to shame'" (Romans 10:9-11).

Ask that individual to read a verse aloud and then have them explain the verse to you. Take them through all the verses listed above.

If the individual interprets a passage incorrectly, do not argue or offer your interpretation, but politely ask him to read it again, and then explain it a second time.

Misinterpretation should not be much of a problem if you use the Bible verses listed above.

Even if your friend mentions that he does not believe in or agree with the Bible, it is best not to argue.

You can state that you simply want him to understand what the Bible says about eternity.

CROSS-CULTURAL DISCIPLE MAKING

Cross-cultural disciple making is an essential aspect of spreading the gospel to unreached populations all over the world.

Christians are called to bridge the gaps between various cultures, so that proper connections can be made to share the message of Jesus Christ.

Embarking on this journey can be both challenging and rewarding, and intentional, especially as the evangelist plan and prepare for your cross-cultural mission trip.

They must consider how best to use the time and resources available, not forgetting knowing what strategies they could employ to effectively engage in evangelism, and by taking an intentional approach to disciple making, the evangelist can maximize the impact of their trip, and more effectively reach out to people in need.

Evangelism requires a conscious effort (John 4:4; Acts 16:13). As disciples, we must be deliberate in our approach to sharing the gospel, particularly when faced with cross- cultural challenges. (John 4:4) ⁴ Now he had to go through Samaria; (Acts 16:13)¹³ On the Sabbath we went outside the city gate to the river, where we expected to find a place of prayer. We sat down and began to speak to the women who had gathered there.

The Evangelist will learn as they go, they will stay open to learning about others, themselves, and the Holy Spirit's works. They must have a genuine interest in others, and seek to understand them; being flexible, adapting your approach when necessary, and listen to the Holy Spirit's guidance (Prov. 18:13). [13] To answer before listening that is folly and shameful.

The evangelist must embrace mistakes; it is understood that no one likes to make mistakes, but that is a part of the learning process.

In certain cases, the evangelist can accept failure, and use it as an opportunity to grow, also by accepting that mistakes will occur, the evangelist must trust that the Holy Spirit will work through your shortcomings, and learn from their errors, apologize, and move forward.

The evangelist must identify God's bridges. The purpose of a bridge is designed to connect two places that were separated. In disciple making, they should seek out the bridges God has already constructed between cultures for God creates social opportunities for sharing the gospel (John 4:39).

Leverage these relationships to spread the gospel more effectively where the evangelist must share the gospel with everyone, and pay particular interest on those who are most receptive (Acts 18:5–8).

They must Focus on building relationships with those who show interest and openness to the gospel message, and regardless of the level of receptivity, the evangelist must stay committed to being authentic and honest about their faith (Romans 12:10- 18). [10] Be devoted to one another in love. Honor one another above yourselves. [11] Never be lacking in zeal, but keep your spiritual fervor, serving the Lord. [12] Be joyful in hope, patient in affliction, faithful in prayer. [13] Share with the Lord's people who are in need. Practice hospitality. [14] Bless those who persecute you; bless and do not curse. [15] Rejoice with those who rejoice; mourn with those who mourn. [16] Live in harmony with one another. Do not be proud, but be willing to associate with people of low position.[a] Do not be conceited.

[17] Do not repay anyone evil for evil. Be careful to do what is right in the eyes of everyone. [18] If it is possible, as far as it depends on you, live at peace with everyone.

The evangelist should be praying without ceasing, which means setting aside time each day to pray for yourself, those you are engaging with, and the spiritual growth of all involved.

They should pray for themselves; they should ask others to pray for you (Col. 4:3–4) and pray for those with whom you are sharing the gospel. (Colossians 4:3-4)[3] And pray for everyone, that God may open a door for our message, so that we may proclaim the mystery of Christ, for which I am in chains. 4 Pray that I may proclaim it clearly, as I should. (Colossians 4:3-4)[3] And pray for us, too, that God may open a door for our message, so that we may proclaim the mystery of Christ, for which I am in chains. [4] Pray that I may proclaim it clearly, as I should.

The evangelist must establish a connection by finding common ground to foster gospel conversations. Jesus and early disciples met people where they were in their spiritual journeys (Acts 8:30). They must engage in discussions about hometowns, food, family, or sports, and participate in tea or coffee rituals to create opportunities for gospel conversations.

The evangelist must proclaim the gospel for their goal is to guide others toward repentance and faith in Jesus (Acts 20:21), and while learning about other cultures and building relationships is valuable, they must remember that salvation comes through the gospel message, not our friendships or influence. (Acts 20:21) [21] I have declared to both Jews and Greeks that they must turn to God in repentance and have faith in our Lord Jesus.

The evangelist must cultivate cultural sensitivity by the time to research and understand the customs, beliefs, and values of the people with whom you are engaging. (1 Corinthians 9:19- 23) Paul's Use of His Freedom -[19] Though I am free and belong to no one, I have made myself a slave to everyone, to win as many as possible. [20] To the Jews I became like a Jew, to win the Jews. To those under the law I became like one under the law (though I myself am not under the law), so as to win those under the law. [21] To those not having the law I became like one not having the law (though I am not free from God's law but am under Christ's law), so as to win those not having the law. [22] To the weak I became weak, to win the weak. I have become all things to all people so that by all possible means I might save some. [23] I do all this for the sake of the gospel, that I may share in its blessings.

This will help them avoid unintentional offenses, and demonstrate respect for their culture.

By showing genuine interest, and appreciation for their traditions, the evangelist can build trust, thereby creating a more conducive environment for sharing the gospel message.

Their goal is to effectively communicate the love of Christ, and being culturally sensitive which allows the evangelist to do so in a way that truly resonates with others.

The evangelist must make disciples by expanding the reach of the gospel, and share the love of Christ with people from diverse backgrounds. As they embark on this journey, they must remember the importance of intentionality, learning, humility, prayer, and cultural sensitivity.

They should effectively navigate the complexities of cross- cultural evangelism, and make a lasting impact on the lives of others. It is through the power of the Holy Spirit and our obedience to God's call that we can bring the life-changing message of Jesus Christ to the ends of the earth. Embrace this calling and watch as God works through you to transform lives for His glory.

DIGITAL AND SOCIAL MEDIA EVANGELISM

I learn that prior to 2019 when it comes to evangelism it was mainly done via face to face contact; knocking on doors; giving out tracks with biblical messages; and hard copy invitation, ad during this time digital and social media was place on the back burner because it was seen ,as no importance other than proclaiming Jesus Christ, and focusing on overseas mission.

In 2019 there became a drastic change where people were dying rapidly all over the world, digital, and social media became an household name, and a life line for many, and since no one was prepared for what was to come many church leaders began to scramble to find various ways on how to reach there congregation, which are still being refined today.

Many churches scrambled to come to life, but to no avail many of their door closed leaving may people stranded when it came to attending church, and I must say that I gave great respect to the church leader that's despite their responsibility to their immediate family, they were responsible for every church member also this was a great responsibility.

Most people did not believe the seriousness of what was happening, and many of them died, and those alive had to find ways to link up with their church members, and how to help them say in believing in God, and For those who survive this ordeal, they are still alive, and are trying to find the best way to draw soles to Jesus Christ.

The digital and social media have become a household name, and a lifeline to many, and when it came to evangelism, there became a significant transformation in recent years, which propelled by rapid technological.

Technology became very important when it came to the gospel message, it build online communities that foster genuine relationships, and spiritual growth, and digital evangelism became popular.

The Power of Digital Evangelism

In evangelism, digital platforms, it possess a power to reach a global audience with the life-transforming message of the Gospel, allowing to connect with individuals from diverse cultures, backgrounds, and locations.

Through social media, websites, and other digital channels, churches and ministries can engage with people who may never be able encountered the Gospel, and it enables them to reach people regardless of the distance.

Regardless of the distance, disabilities, or societal restrictions, the digital age provided an inclusive environment, where individuals can freely explore their faith, and encounter God's love.

Additionally, digital evangelism fosters the creation of online communities where believers can connect, share their experiences, support one another, and build meaningful relationships grounded in faith.

Through these communities, discipleship and spiritual growth can flourish, extending the reach of our ministry far beyond the confines of physical gatherings.

Understanding the Digital Mission Field

I learn "To effectively engage in digital evangelism, it is important to have a comprehensive understanding of the digital mission field.

The constant update and demand of digital culture today cannot be ignored. People increasingly turn to the internet and digital platforms for information, connection, and spiritual exploration."

By recognizing the significance of this cultural shift, one can strategically position themselves to meet people where they are, in the digital space where there is this constant demand of needs and challenges of online seekers.

Many individuals in the digital realm seek answers, hope, and purpose but need more personal connections to overcome obstacles such as skepticism, information overload, and a lack of personal connection is hard to get use of.

Navigating the diverse range of digital platforms and tools available can be overwhelming, but it presents many opportunities, which is from social media platforms to video- sharing sites, and each platform offers its advantages, and strategies for reaching and engaging with individuals in meaningful ways.

By navigating this digital landscape with intention and discernment, the churches can effectively share the Gospel and make a lasting impact.

Principles for Effective Digital Evangelism

First and foremost, authenticity and transparency in online interactions are vital for effective digital evangelism requires adhering to certain principles that enable us to connect meaningfully with online audiences.

Genuine expressions of faith, vulnerability, and personal experiences resonate with individuals seeking authenticity in a world filled with superficiality.

Cultivating a listening, and empathetic mindset allows one to understand online seekers' unique needs and struggles. By actively listening to their concerns and responding with empathy.

The evangelist can create a safe space for dialogue and exploration of faith, and adapting the message for digital contexts is essential.

The digital realm demands concise, engaging, and visually compelling content that captures attention amid countless distractions.

It is crucial to present the timeless truths of the Gospel in a way that is accessible and relevant to the online audience.

Engaging with relevant and meaningful content on the social media helps build connections and fosters ongoing engagement where the evangelist can encourage people to share their program.

They can got to the extent of addressing the questions, doubts, and issues that online seekers want where they can demonstrate the relevance of the Gospel to their lives.

Building trust and credibility is very important in digital evangelism. Being consistent and having an online presence, timely responses, and reliable information contribute to building trustworthiness.

When embodying these principles, the churches and ministries can effectively convey the message of hope and salvation to a digitally connected world.

Leveraging Digital Tools for Evangelism

Digital tools offer many opportunities to extend the evangelistic efforts where the social media platforms which become a powerful tool for evangelism, allowing the evangelist to share inspiring content, and engaging in conversations, and connect with individuals from diverse backgrounds, not forgetting to find out what is best for the various countries they are reaching out to.

Live streaming and video content creation provide immersive and dynamic ways to communicate the Gospel message, enabling the evangelist to engage with audiences in real time and reach those who prefer visual mediums.

Podcasts, and audio resources offer a convenient and accessible format for sharing teachings, sermons, and testimonies, allowing individuals to engage with faith-related content while on the go.

Online communities, and forums provide spaces for people to connect, ask questions, and explore their faith in a supportive and interactive environment.

Mobile apps and websites are digital hubs for accessing resources, Bible studies, devotionals, and prayer networks.

By comparing and evaluating the digital tools strategically, we can meet people where they are, engage with them in meaningful ways, and create opportunities for them to encounter the life- transforming message of the Gospel.

Building an Effective Digital Evangelism Strategy

A well-thought-out strategy is one of the best tools in the digital evangelism. This involves several key elements which includes:

Defining clear goals, and identifying the target audience is crucial.

Understanding who the evangelist aim to reach and what outcomes they desire. This will help them to tailor their approach and messages effectively.

Creating, engaging, and relevant content is also important. This is done by understanding their target audience's needs, interests, and questions.

They can develop content that captures their attention, and resonates with their hearts.

When using analytics, and data, it will provide valuable insights into the effectiveness of the digital evangelism efforts.

Monitoring metrics such as engagement and conversion rates would enable the evangelist to make wise decision, and allowing them to make wise decision, allows them to adapt various strategies for a more significant impact.

Collaboration with like-minded individuals, and organizations will strengthen the evangelist's digital evangelism efforts.

Partnering with others who share a joint mission would expand evangelism which would encourage mutual support, and fosters a sense of community among those engaged on online ministry.

By implementing these elements, the evangelist can build a robust, and effective digital evangelism strategy that would effectively shares the message of the Gospel and transform many lives.

The Role of Personal Discipleship in the Digital Age

In the digital age, personal discipleship plays a vital role in nurturing, and growing the faith of online seekers who may simply browse the webs, and social media.

Through the digital platforms, the evangelist have the opportunity to establish, and cultivate online relationships for discipleship such as outreach, and missions.

This involves providing guidance, answering questions, and encouraging individuals as they embark on their spiritual journey.

It is important to emphasize the value of offline connections, and those who do not know how to operate the social media function, and only know how to operate a cell phone.

Face-to-face interactions, mentoring relationships, and local church involvement is essential for holistic spiritual growth should not be ignored.

Additionally, providing resources and support for spiritual growth is crucial in the digital age. Sharing relevant Bible studies, devotionals, and teaching materials can empower individuals to deepen their understanding of God's Word and applying it to their lives.

Integrating personal discipleship into our digital evangelism efforts can create a nurturing environment where online seekers can find guidance, develop meaningful connections, and experience transformative growth.

Embracing the opportunities of digital evangelism is essential in reaching and impacting a digitally connected world.

As the evangelist recognize the power of digital platforms, they can strive and increase boundaries.

This is overcoming limitations, and amplifying the impact of the gospel message, and the power of the gospel remains constant, regardless if it is in the digital environment or face to face.

The word of God will always touch hearts, which will always transform lives, and bringing hope to those searching the media a special peace of mind.

As the evangelist engage in digital evangelism, those who are viewing , they will be encourage to invite others to spread the Good News online.

Together, everyone can harness the potential of technology, leverage digital tools, and build genuine connections that lead people closer to God.

Embrace this digital era with creativity, authenticity, and not forgetting face to face contact people will have a deep conviction to share the message of God's love and salvation, bringing hope, and spreading the gospel beyond the four walls of the Church is needed all over the world.

Overcoming Challenges and Pitfalls

While the digital evangelism opens exciting possibilities, it also presents many difficult challenges, and potential pitfalls that will constantly be there will is to maintain proper navigation while using wisdom and discernment.

One popular challenge is finding the right balance between virtual and physical connections.

While digital platforms offer opportunities for evangelism engagement, it is important to encourage offline connections and face-to-face interactions whenever possible, for this will foster a deeper relationships and discipleship.

Addressing the issue of online is another challenge. There must be a way for creating safe and trustworthy online spaces.

It is crucial while being aware that some individuals are there to discourage the gospel to be shown, and one has to be mindful of this.

Dealing with misinformation and digital distractions requires discernment and vigilance.

As the churches. and ministries navigate the digital landscape, they must ensure that they shared content is accurate, grounded in truth, and aligned with biblical principles.

The evangelist must guard against superficiality, and shallow engagement that often characterize online interactions.

By fostering meaningful conversations, encouraging depth of thought, and promoting intentional engagement, the evangelist can overcome these challenges and foster genuine connections that lead to spiritual growth and transformation.

Evangelism	Healing
Telling people who aren't Christians about Jesus Eph 4:11	Asking God to heal people 1 Cor 12:9
Prophecy	**Miracles**
Encouraging people by telling them how God sees things 1 Cor 12:10	Asking God to use his power to do amazing things 1 Cor 12:10
Teaching	**Faith**
Teaching people about God in a way they can understand Romans 12:7	Trusting God to do certain things 1 Cor 12:9
Speaking in tongues	**Apostles**
Speaking unknown languages to help encourage others of pray (someone else can interpret) 1 Cor 12:10	Finding new and different ways of doing God's work Eph 4:11
Service	**Wisdom**
Helping others to do God's work 1 Cor 12:28	Understanding situations and how God would want things to be done 1 Cor 12:8

Additional informatin that can benefit the evangelist

NICENE CREED

The Nicene Creed is a statement of faith dating early in church history and was used to protect believers against heresy. It is a carefully crafted statement that conveys the basic tenants of Christianity and was later used as a prayer.

The prayer includes the following beliefs: belief in the Holy Spirit, the Lord, the giver of life, who proceeds from the Father and the Son, who with the Father and the Son is adored and glorified, who has spoken through the prophets; belief in one, holy, catholic and apostolic Church; and confession of one Baptism for the forgiveness of sins.

The prayer ends with a confession of faith in the resurrection of the dead and the life of the world to come:

"I believe in one God, the Father almighty, maker of heaven and earth, of all things visible and invisible. I believe in one Lord Jesus Christ, the Only Begotten Son of God, born of the Father before all ages. God from God, Light from Light, true God from true God, begotten, not made, consubstantial with the Father; through him all things were made.

For us men and for our salvation he came down from heaven, and by the Holy Spirit was incarnate of the Virgin Mary and became man. For our sake he was crucified under Pontius Pilate, he suffered death and was buried and rose again on the third day in accordance with the Scriptures.

He ascended into heaven and is seated at the right hand of the Father. He will come again in glory to judge the living and the dead and his kingdom will have no end.

I believe in the Holy Spirit, the Lord, the giver of life, who proceeds from the Father and the Son, who with the Father and the Son is adored and glorified, who has spoken through the prophets.

I believe in one, holy, catholic and apostolic Church. I confess one Baptism for the forgiveness of sins, and I look forward to the resurrection of the dead and the life of the world to come." Amen

THE LORD'S PRAYER (PSALM 23)

Our Father who art in heaven,
hallowed be thy name.
Thy kingdom come.
Thy will be done
on earth as it is in heaven.
Give us this day our daily bread,
and forgive us our trespasses,
as we forgive those who trespass against us,
and lead us not into temptation,
but deliver us from evil.
For thine is the kingdom and the power, and the glory,
forever and ever.
Amen.

ADDITIONAL QUESTION THE EVANGELIST CAN USE TO EVANGELIZE

I've made it my lifelong goal to learn from others; what's the greatest lesson you feel you've learned so far in your life's journey?

Tell me about your greatest success and your greatest failure along the way.

Would you mind sharing with me the greatest piece of wisdom ever passed on to you?

What prompted you to pursue your career in ? What do you like most about what you do? least?

Do you see this as a lifetime career, or a steppingstone to something else?

If someone wanted to talk to you about God, how would you like to be approached?

Have you ever had anyone approach you and try to talk to you about God?

What kinds of feelings were you left with after the encounter?

What images or words come to your mind when you hear the word evangelism?

The word evangelism means "to proclaim good news." If that's true, why do you think this word carries so much baggage with it?

If you were asked to describe the good news that evangelists are supposed to be sharing with people, how would you describe it?

What is your dream job?

Are you working toward it already? If not, what is standing in your way?

What advice would you give to a young person about finding vocational happiness?

What kind of exposure did you have to religion when you were growing up?

Why do you think there are so many different religions?

Do you think it's possible for all religions to be equally right? Why or why not?

What conclusions have you come to concerning life after death?

Do you think it's possible to be certain about where you'll spend eternity?

Have you ever explored what the Bible has to say about eternal life?

Have you ever been able to get a handle on what you think your purpose in life is?

Everyone seems to agree that money by itself can't buy happiness. What, in your opinion, does guarantee a happy life?

In what ways do you feel you're really winning or losing life? Do you consider yourself to be a Christian?

Based on your understanding, how does someone become a Christian?

Have you ever explored what the Bible has to say about how someone becomes a Christian?

As you've watched or read the news, what conclusions have you drawn about the nature of humanity?

Do you believe there is a solution to social problems such as rape, murder, famine, war, racism, and divorce?

Have you ever had an experience in which you felt the presence of evil?

Have you ever had an experience in which you felt the presence of God?

In what ways have you seen good and evil played out in your life?

What causes you to struggle the most with the idea of God's existence?

Up to this point in your life's journey, have you met anyone or experienced anything that made the reality of God seem plausible to you?

To what do you attribute your disbelief in God?

It sounds as if you value open-mindedness. Do you ever find yourself closing your mind to certain things, ideas, or people?

What criteria do you use to determine whether something is true?

Does your worldview allow for any absolutes? How did you meet your husband/wife?

What have you learned about yourself through marriage? What do you enjoy most about marriage? least?

Has your understanding of the word love changed over the years?

Why do you think so many couples end up falling out of love?

If you could pass along one word of advice about how to keep a relationship going and growing, what would it be?

Why do you think so many people prefer to live as if God does not exist?

What would you want God to do to validate his existence and bring you to belief?

It's been said that many people never find God for the same reason a robber can't find the policeman standing on the corner; what does this saying mean to you?

Some people believe that we are the product of a random evolutionary process. Do you think discussions about right and wrong have a place in that kind of worldview?

How do/will you teach your kids right from wrong?

What authority do you appeal to?

Did you have any dreams or set any life goals when you were younger?

What dreams have you let go of?

What dreams are you still hanging on to?

Are you optimistic or pessimistic about the future of our world?

Do you think it's easier or harder to raise kids in today's world than it was when you were growing up?

What concerns you most when you think about your future? What experiences have shaped your worldview the most?

Has there been one book or movie that's left its mark on you in a significant way? How so?

Besides your parents, is there any one person, who stands out as having had a major role in shaping your life?

Tell me about him or her. God has changed my life; have you ever considered letting him change yours?

If God had his way with you, what do you think he would change first?

What scares you the most about letting God change your life?

What three principles of life have benefited you the most so far in your life's journey?

What, if anything, causes you to be hopeful about your future?

If you had only six months to live, what would be on your list of things to do before you died? Why?

As people get to know you, what about you do they enjoy most? As people get to know you, what about you do they enjoy least?

As people get to know you, in what area do you feel most misunderstood?

How would you describe your leadership style? What leadership style do you respond best to?

Jesus was described as a servant leader. When have you, if ever, experienced that kind of leadership?

Why do you do what you do?

What life experiences have molded you and motivated you to pursue the path you've chosen for life?

If you were to choose your path over again, would you choose the same one? Why or why not?

If you could ask God three questions, what would you ask?

If God were to ask this one question, "Are you for me or against me?" what would you say?

What evidence would you present to defend your response? Which gender do you think has the tougher path in life?

What do you enjoy most about the opposite sex? What do you enjoy most about being male/female? Have you ever hated anyone?

Has anyone ever hated you?

Have you ever been able to overcome hatred? If so, how did you pull it off?

If you could choose the manner of your death, how would you like to go?

How would you like to be remembered at your funeral? Does the thought of death scare you?

It's been said that life is largely out of our control. If that's true, why do so many people try to control the uncontrollable?

Do you struggle with trying to control things?

What kinds of things do you think can be controlled in life? What kinds of habits do you struggle with most?

Do you ever find yourself doing the very things you don't want to do, or not doing the things you really want to do? If so, what do you attribute this to?

Have you ever found anything to set you free from this cycle?

How would you change the way you were raised?

What things are you doing/going to do to raise your kids differently?

What values from your childhood do you want to pass on to your kids?

If Jesus were here right now, what would you ask him? How do you think he would answer?

How would you feel if that happened?

The Benefits of Evangelism

Personal Transformation – which is through evangelism, individuals often experience changes in beliefs, attitudes, and behaviors. They might find new purpose, joy, and peace in life, aligning their actions more closely with the teachings of Jesus Christ.

Family Relationships - The Christian teachings of love, forgiveness, and patience can transform familial relationships, promoting more harmony and understanding within households.

Emotional Healing - Many people experience emotional healing as they encounter the message of God's love and forgiveness, sometimes finding release from guilt, shame, anger, or bitterness.

Freedom from Addictions - The power of faith, prayer, and supportive community often helps individuals overcome various addictions, leading to healthier and more productive lives.

Societal Impact - Evangelism can lead to positive societal changes, as new believers often become more compassionate, generous, and committed to justice and service in their communities.

Educational Advancement - In many instances, the church community encourages and supports educational pursuits, leading to improved life outcomes for many individuals Economic Improvement- As people experience personal transformation and grow in responsibility, integrity, and work ethic, this can lead to economic improvements at both the individual and community levels.

Leadership Development - As individuals grow in their faith, they often develop leadership skills that can benefit not only their church community, but also their workplace, family, and broader society.

Evangelism helps keep the gospel central in our lives and churches – This is because the evangelist must be always in the word which keeps them on their toes.

Evangelism deepens our understanding of the most fundamental truths of Scripture – this is due to studying and learning how to approach evangelize in the right manner and having that thirst to do the work of the Lord.

Properly motivated evangelism grows our love for God and neighbor – This is done through finding way to evangelism.

Evangelism prompts unexpected questions and objections from non-Christians, which can deepen our faith – This is due to the interaction between the evangelist and the people they are ministering to.

Evangelism protects us from mistakenly assuming that those around us are saved – The behavior of the unsaved are different and being the true evangelist they are.

Evangelism Helps Keep the Gospel Central in ones lives and churches

Gospel conversations with non-Christians' force one to better grasp the central, underpinning truths of God's Word. Issues like God's character, his holiness and wrath, man's creation in God's image, sin, grace, the cross of Christ, and judgment all come into sharp focus.

One have to think through explaining these concepts to different people in different circumstances, and one learn better how these truths lace together all of Scripture from Genesis to Revelation.

One of the clearest verses on the discipleship benefits of evangelism is Philemon 1:6: "I pray that you may be active in sharing your faith, so that you will have a full understanding of every good thing we have in Christ."

Knowing something and explaining it to someone who doesn't understand it or believe it are two different things. These treasured truths become clearer to us as we explain them to others.

Properly Motivated Evangelism Grows Our Love for God and Neighbor

All people are called to wholeheartedly love God and other people (Mark 12:28–31). Sharing our faith because we love God and people stokes the fire of this love all the more. I've never seen properly motivated evangelism do the opposite.

Evangelism Protects Us from Mistakenly Assuming That Those Around you are Saved.

Not being careful about who we consider to be "born again" often has its roots in unbiblical views of conversion.

The sower spread the seed liberally, seemingly without consideration for where it landed (path, rocks, thorns, soil; Mark 4:2–8).

We too should share the gospel broadly and without discrimination, allowing our sovereign God to use it however he sees fit, to save the lost as well as encourage the saints.

Evangelism Increases the Likelihood of Being Persecuted for the Gospel, Which Leads to Our Growth.

Some hinderances of Evangelizing

I learn that too many Christians and believers fail to be compassionate, and Christ-like to others, while in the church they are friendly, but out of the church thy behavior is different, and this action can prevent them from sharing the gospel.

Most church ministries are not intentionally evangelistic; some people may feel that it is not their place to go beyond the four walls of the church to invite anyone.

Some accept the position by pretending to the Pastor that they are evangelic inclined, when they are not, and this is one of the key reason why many people will attend the church and walk out, some of them do not know how to treat people, they would embrace them the first couple of times the visitors which they did not invite arrive at the church, then abruptly they become cold, and distant.

Evangelism can be seen as manipulative, corrupting or intolerant of treat beliefs, or as assuming that one is better than everyone else, for this is because those who are evangelizing behave in a manner as if they are better than those they are evangelizing to.

Evangelism can fail to honor has unique persons especially if the people are of different nationality, the color of the skin, sex orientation, the way they look. In most cases evangelist behavior is unwarranted, which would wonder if the evangelist were really saved, or is allowing envy and jealousy to overcome them.

According to Mr. Gary McIntosh, there are additional barriers to evangelism. Hopefully, churches would recognize some of the barriers, and they will take action to eliminate them.

In some cases, the new churches are usually much more effective at winning new people to faith in Christ, but when the church became older churches, for many reasons, as a church grows older, it develops barriers that keep it from making new disciples.

The major barrier is the low commitment to personal evangelism found in the members and regular worshippers of a church. Are a church's individual members sharing their faith with friends, acquaintances, and family members?

Or are they neglecting such activity? In newer churches, between two-thirds to three-fourths of the people first attend due to the invitation of a friend or family member. As these new people get involved, they enthusiastically share their faith with other people with whom they come into contact. As this early enthusiasm wanes, the evangelistic potential of a church declines.

Related to this is the low evangelistic conscience found in many churches. The focus of sermons on biblical knowledge, historical events, and modern issues often comes with a reduced emphasis on the need for salvation.

Another way to state it is, the recent emphasis on the Great Commandment often comes with a reduced emphasis on the Great Commission. Unless the fact of the lostness of mankind is preached passionately from the pulpit, a church is not likely to be passionate about evangelism.

Another barrier is where there is little training for evangelism in most churches. Churches tend to get results related to the training and teaching they offer. It is not surprising that churches, which train their members to share the gospel, get the best evangelistic results.

It is not surprising that churches weak in evangelism rarely train and teach members to evangelize. Studies demonstrate that evangelistic churches train a minimum of 10% of their people yearly to share their faith.

A misunderstanding between the words *outreach* and *evangelism* creates another barrier. Outreach is any ministry that connects a church with its non churched community.

When a church reaches into its community with missional acts of service (e.g., food distribution, job counseling, divorce recovery, etc.), it is doing outreach. In contrast, evangelism takes place when non-Christians are challenged to place their personal faith in Jesus Christ alone for salvation.

The problem is that many churches are doing outreach but not evangelism. But, since they do not understand the difference, many churches think they are active evangelistically, but they are not.

Most churches focus on being friendly rather than being friends to newcomers. While it is true that guests to our churches want a friendly welcome, long term what they really seek are friends.

When guests encounter a friendly church they naturally expect that they will be able to make lots of friends. Unfortunately, it is easier in most churches to become a member than to make lasting friendships.

Since most people come to Christ through family and friend connections, this lack of friend-making in churches leads to fewer people accepting Christ as their personal savior.

Related to the lack of friend making is the inability of churches to assimilate newcomers into areas of service. Churches tend to have few entry level places of service for newcomers.

In addition most of the available areas require high verbal skills. Newcomers who are not competent with speaking tend to find few places of service.

Churches that do well in evangelism offer numerous places where people with nonverbal skills may be involved (craft groups, work projects, mission trips, etc.).

The lack of seeker events is another reason for the low level of evangelism in many churches. Churches that effectively reach new people for Christ offer from four to eight events each year aimed primarily at reaching non-Christians.

A great danger for the church today is assuming the salvation of people who simply claim the label "Christian" or are involved in church activities.

Word of Caution when comes to Evangelizing

As one evangelizes, they have to be reminded of the reasons why they are evangelizing.

When evangelizing, it is crucial to focus on discipleship and the lasting impact of faith, not just on the initial conversion.

Additionally, be mindful of how your words and actions might be perceived by others, especially those who may not initially be receptive to the gospel.

As one push forward in evangelism as a part of their discipleship, be careful with evangelistic programs.

One must not treat evangelism as a program, but as a ministry.

Encouragement

The greatest encouragement to your congregation, and Christian friends to be actively sharing their faith is for the senior pastor and elders to be seen and heard sharing their faith. People will learn best what you are most excited about.

If you as a pastor are excited to share your faith, the congregation will learn to be excited to share their faith. And they will grow as disciples of Jesus as they do.

Jesus told his apostles in the Great Commission, "Make disciples...teaching them to observe all that I have commanded you" (Matt. 28:19).

As we make disciples, let's be sure to model and teach them all that he commanded, including the great joy and blessing of a life of evangelism.

CONCLUSION

One may not believe but Evangelists are partly responsible for the Christian lives of the people that they share the gospel with because they are the one whose words that penetrate the hearts and mind of those they are ministering to.

Their words of encourage of coming to Christ or surrendering one's life to Christ that they listen to thereby grabbing their attention to want to know more about Jesus Christ and having that desire to want to visit the church to hear more about Jesus Christ.

An Evangelist must be saved by the Lord, and when they are ministering to the people it must be done in spirit and in truth, so those who are listening will want to know more because they will have a positive expectation when they attend church.

The evangelist will and must make sure that when that person arrives at church, they will be welcome, and must be treated as a newborn baby, at least for a while, if not, after a while that person will become discouraged and never return.

An Evangelist must minister to those in a way God want them to, and when doing so they will see the success which is a true servant a servant of God who carries out God's will, worships God as seen like Abraham

That night the LORD appeared to him and said, "I am the God of your father Abraham. Do not be afraid, for I am with you; I will bless you and will increase the number of your descendants for the sake of my servant Abraham." (Genesis 26:2) [2] The Lord appeared to Isaac and said, "Do not go down to Egypt; live in the land where I tell you to live.

Moses mentioned in [31] And when the Israelites saw the mighty hand of the Lord displayed against the Egyptians, the people feared the Lord and put their trust in him and in Moses his servant (Exodus 14:31); [5] And Moses the servant of the Lord died there in Moab, as the Lord had said and Deuteronomy 34:5.

David: (2 Samuel 7:5); [5] "Go and tell my servant David, 'This is what the Lord says: Are you the one to build me a house to dwell in? (2 Samuel 7:8)[8] "Now then, tell my servant David, 'This is what the Lord Almighty says; I took you from the pasture, from tending the flock, and appointed you ruler over my people Israel. and Isaiah: Mentioned in Isaiah 20:3 [3] Then the Lord said, "Just as my servant Isaiah has gone stripped and barefoot for three years, as a sign and portent against Egypt and Cush; Paul: Titus 1:1 "1 Paul, a servant of God and an apostle of Jesus Christ to further the faith of God's elect and their knowledge of the truth that leads to godliness; James: Mentioned in James 1:1 "1 James, a servant of God and of the Lord Jesus Christ, To the twelve tribes scattered among the nations" and they are those are being devoted and helpful, being humble before God, being ready to act when God inspires or nudges, helping others meet their needs, not being motivated by money or reward, living to fulfill God's will, rejecting actions that go against God's rule, being devoted to doing good and walking in the Spirit, servant of the Lord Meaning, and in conclusion - God's servants were those who worshiped him and carried out his will, often in important leadership roles.

The book of Psalms 118:15-25 "15 Shouts of joy and victory resound in the tents of the righteous: "The LORD's right hand has done mighty things!16 The LORD's right hand is lifted high; the LORD's right hand has done mighty things!"17 I will not die but live, and will proclaim what the LORD has done. The Lord has chastened me severely, but he has not given me over to death. Open for me the gates of the righteous; I will enter and give thanks to the Lord. This is the gate of the Lord through which the righteous may enter.

I will give you thanks, for you answered me; you have become my salvation. The stone the builders rejected has become the cornerstone; the Lord has done this, and it is marvelous in our eyes. The Lord has done it this very day; let us rejoice today and be glad. Lord, save us! Lord, grant us success!

Bible says a wise man wins souls proverbs 11:30 30 The fruit of the righteous is a tree of life, and he that Winnett souls is wise.

REFERENCES

Holy Bible

Barriers to Evangelism - The Good Book Blog - Biola University; Gary McIntosh

99 Wondering Questions | Cru https://www.cru.org/us/en/ communities

Charles Spurgeon; https://www.ministrybrands.com/ https://growahealthychurch.com/

Harnessing Digital Tools for Evangelism: A Guide for Churches - Church Communications Group; https://churchcommunications.com/

Harnessing Digital Tools for Evangelism: A Guide for Churches (Katie Allred)

Dr. Sharon Forde-Atikossie -A bird with a Broken Wing Dr. Sharon Forde-Atikossie - Missionary Onboard!

Paul Chilcote- The Study of Evangelism: Exploring a Missional Practice of the Church Paperback

David Geisler Conversational Evangelism: Connecting with People to Share Jesus Paperback

www.ingramcontent.com/pod-product-compliance
Lightning Source LLC
Chambersburg PA
CBHW051233120626
46547CB00013B/1620